MYSTERIES OF THE ROSARY

for Seniors

Dennis H. Ference

Liguori

Imprimi Potest:
Richard Thibodeau, CSsR
Provincial, Denver Province
The Redemptorists

Imprimatur:
Most Reverend Michael J. Sheridan
Auxiliary Bishop, Archdiocese of St. Louis

INTRODUCTION

The rosary holds an honored place in the prayer life of many elders. Its unaltered, common form weaves a stable thread throughout a lifetime lived in a world of rapid and ongoing change. At a time when memories play a valuable role in reminding the elder of the graces of a life's journey, the rosary is a rich symbol of one's religious heritage.

The rosary offers simplicity and familiarity in its patterns and repetitions. At the same time it provides, through the mysteries, a window to the great events and truths of the faith.

Reflecting on these truths helps us to encounter God in familiar yet sometimes surprising ways.

The mysteries of our faith have the power to transform the happenings of human life and give them new meaning and sacredness. The prayers in this booklet aim to help you, the reader, experience aging and its realities in the light of God's dealings with the people of God as presented in the Joyful, Sorrowful, Glorious and Luminous Mysteries of the rosary.

As you pray each mystery with the help of this booklet, read the Scripture passage slowly and deliberately. Be open to the power of the words to inspire, challenge, and surprise. Let them speak to you as you are on this particular day. Use the reflection given to help you draw parallels and make connections between what you experience and the words of Scripture. Take from it a sense of God's activity in your life and carry that sense through to the next mystery. End your time of prayer with thanks for the wonder of God's intimate love for us.

HOW TO PRAY
THE ROSARY

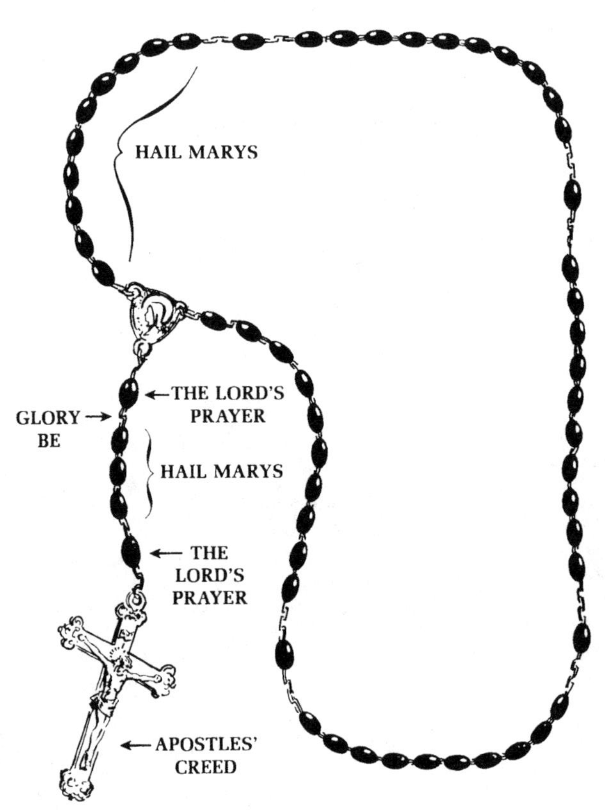

HAIL MARYS
THE LORD'S PRAYER
GLORY BE
HAIL MARYS
THE LORD'S PRAYER
APOSTLES' CREED

The Cross

Begin with the Sign of the Cross and the Apostles' Creed.

The Five Introductory Beads

Pray the Lord's Prayer on the first large bead and a Hail Mary on each of the next three beads. Pray the Doxology on the fifth bead.

The Decades

Announce the mystery, for example, "The Annunciation." (Optional: Read the Scripture verse and meditation for the mystery.) Pray the Lord's Prayer on the large bead. Then pray a Hail Mary on each of the ten smaller beads. The Doxology follows each decade.

Continue throughout the five or all twenty decades, meditating briefly on each mystery.

THE PRAYERS OF THE ROSARY

The Sign of the Cross

In the name of the Father, and of the Son, and of the Holy Spirit. Amen.

The Apostles' Creed

I believe in God, the Father almighty, creator of heaven and earth. I believe in Jesus Christ, his only Son, our Lord. He was conceived by the power of the Holy Spirit and born of the Virgin Mary. He suffered under Pontius Pilate, was crucified, died, and was buried. He descended into hell. On the third day he rose again. He ascended into heaven and is seated at the right hand of the Father. He will come again to judge the living and the dead. I believe in the Holy Spirit, the holy catholic Church, the communion of saints, the forgiveness of sins, the resurrection of the body, and life everlasting. Amen.

The Lord's Prayer

Our Father, who art in heaven, hallowed be thy name; thy kingdom come; thy will be done on earth as it is in heaven. Give us this day our daily bread; and forgive us our trespasses, as we forgive those who trespass against us; and lead us not into temptation, but deliver us from evil. Amen.

The Hail Mary

Hail Mary, full of grace. The Lord is with thee. Blessed art thou among women, and blessed is the fruit of thy womb, Jesus. Holy Mary, Mother of God, pray for us sinners, now and at the hour of our death. Amen.

The Doxology

Glory be to the Father, and to the Son, and to the Holy Spirit, as it was in the beginning, is now, and ever shall be, world without end. Amen.

THE JOYFUL MYSTERIES

THE ANNUNCIATION

The angel said to her, "Do not be afraid, Mary, for you have found favor with God. And now, you will conceive in your womb and bear a son, and you will name him Jesus. He will be great, and will be called the Son of the Most High." (Luke 1:30–32a)

Lord, how challenging to Mary's faith must have been your angel's message that day. In my efforts to serve you, I too have faced many challenges. Sometimes I have been afraid. Often I have struggled with my "yes." Give me the grace, in these later years, to trust you more and more so that, like your Mother, I can answer your invitations to love with a heartfelt, "Be it done to me according to your word."

THE VISITATION

Mary set out and went with haste to a Judean town in the hill country, where she entered the house of Zechariah and greeted Elizabeth. When Elizabeth heard Mary's greeting, the child leaped in her womb. (Luke 1:39–41a)

Mary was with child. Still, she undertook a tiresome journey to meet the needs of another. Lord, I know there are needs all around me, yet sometimes I get preoccupied with my own concerns. But your presence within and among us always encourages us to reach out to one another. Help me to freely share the love I receive. Help me to add to the joy that comes to this world when compassion reigns over self-interest.

THE NATIVITY

While they were there, the time came for her to deliver her child. And she gave birth to her firstborn son and wrapped him in bands of cloth, and laid him in a manger, because there was no place for them in the inn. (Luke 2:6, 7)

Lord, how often have I failed to make room for you because I didn't recognize you in the ordinariness in which you came to me? How often have I passed you by when I ignored the poor, the small, or the sick? How often do I now overlook you in my own wrinkling skin and softening muscles? Open these aging eyes and heart so that I may see and welcome you whenever and however you choose to enter my life.

THE PRESENTATION

When the time came for their purification according to the law of Moses, they brought him up to Jerusalem to present him to the Lord. (Luke 2:22)

Lord, when you were presented in the Temple, who could have known how intimate a relationship you already shared with your Father? I sometimes forget that from my very conception I too was meant to have an intimate relationship with you, my God. And so, I often overlook the immeasurable worth you give me by sharing your very life with me. Help me to stay mindful of my dignity that comes only from you. Inspire me to frequently renew my baptismal "presentation" with a free and loving return to you of all that I have received.

THE FINDING IN THE TEMPLE

When his parents saw him they were astonished; and his mother said to him, "Child, why have you treated us like this?" He said to them, "Why were you searching for me? Did you not know that I must be in my Father's house?" (Luke 2:48a, 49)

Lord, sometimes the things you said and did on this earth puzzle me, so I must dig a little deeper to get to the heart of the matter. That always seems to involve putting God first above everything else—my own ambitions, security, possessions, family. Lord, I don't want to spend my remaining years chasing illusions. Help me to live life fully. Help me get to the heart of the matter.

THE SORROWFUL MYSTERIES

They went to a place called Gethsemane; and he said to his disciples, "Sit here while I pray." He took with him Peter and James and John, and began to be distressed and agitated. And he said to them, "I am deeply grieved, even to death." (Mark 14:32–34a)

Lord, so terrible was your battle with fear and loneliness that night that you sweat blood. I cannot face the losses of aging and the certainty of approaching death without fear. Watch with me, Lord, whenever I am anxious. And whenever I must encounter the cup of suffering, teach me to meet my fears with trust in the mercy and wisdom of your Father.

THE SCOURGING

So Pilate, wishing to satisfy the crowd, released Barabbas for them; and after flogging Jesus, he handed him over to be crucified. (Mark 15:15)

Lord, I cannot imagine the pain you suffered in body, mind, and spirit as the jagged pieces of metal attached to strips of leather tore into your flesh. Most often, the pains of my life are merely an annoyance. But sometimes they cut deep into my very soul and I wonder where I will find the strength to endure. As I age and pain seems to visit more frequently, help me to understand that no one's life is pain free. Help me to unite my sufferings to your passion as an act of love for the salvation of the world.

THE CROWNING WITH THORNS

[The soldiers] clothed him in a purple cloak; and after twisting some thorns into a crown, they put it on him. And they began saluting him, "Hail, King of the Jews!" (Mark 15:16–18)

Lord, how totally you gave up control into the hands of the soldiers as you allowed yourself to become the target for their taunts and cruel torture. It is control that I'm after when I mourn the loss of a youthful appearance, deny the reality of a slowed step, or balk unreasonably at change and new ways of doing things. Lord, help me to understand that the only meaningful control I have comes from my "yes" to you and your plan for my life.

THE CARRYING OF THE CROSS

Carrying the cross by himself, he went out to what is called The Place of the Skull, which in Hebrew is called Golgotha. (John 19:16b, 17)

Lord, the words, "carrying the cross by himself," remind me of the loneliness you must have felt that dreadful day. And there is loneliness in the carrying of all our crosses no matter how many people offer support or encouragement. Yet this lonely task of taking up the cross is what you ask of all who wish to be your followers. Lord, give me comfort and strength by reminding me that in this difficult task of carrying my cross I enter ever more deeply into the mystery of your life and love.

THE CRUCIFIXION

When they came to the place that is called The Skull, they crucified Jesus there with the criminals, one on his right and one on his left. (Luke 23:33)

Lord, thank you for sharing so fully in being human. Thinking about your life helps me give meaning to my life. Reflecting on your death helps me accept the reality of my death. For years death was difficult for me to imagine and seemed so far in the future. That's not so anymore. With each passing year it becomes harder to ignore. And now, as I think about my death, help me to look to the cross and pronounce your words of surrender that will truly make me free: "Father, into your hands I commend My Spirit" (Luke 23:46).

THE GLORIOUS MYSTERIES

THE RESURRECTION

The angel said to the women, "Do not be afraid; I know that you are looking for Jesus who was crucified. He is not here; for he has been raised, as he said. Come, see the place where he lay." (Matthew 28:5–6)

Lord, the women came to see your crucified body. They found, instead, an empty tomb. I have often seen new life coming out of apparent failure. I have experienced exciting possibilities springing from shattered dreams. I've come to understand that, in your creative wisdom, this is the way things were meant to be. Lord, I need to look at death as a gateway to life. Over and over again I need to recall your resurrection and its promise for me.

THE ASCENSION

Then he led them out as far as Bethany, and, lifting up his hands, he blessed them. While he was blessing them, he withdrew from them and was carried up into heaven. (Luke 24:50, 51)

Lord, as with all things in this world, your earthly presence came to an end. But you promised that where you were going, you would prepare a place for your friends. Throughout my life, I have sought the comfort of feeling at home. Yet, I have come to realize that any home in this world will only be temporary. I came from you and am meant to return to you. That is the truth of it. Help me to live my remaining years not tied to what must pass but strongly rooted in you and your promises for my future.

THE DESCENT OF THE HOLY SPIRIT

And suddenly from heaven there came a sound like the rush of a violent wind.... All of them were filled with the Holy Spirit and began to speak in other languages, as the Spirit gave them ability. (Acts 2:2,4)

Lord, how wonderfully the Spirit worked in the lives of your friends. Filled with courage, purpose, and joy they went out to literally change the world. Things seem to have a way of slowing down and settling in after years of living. I believe that much of that is good and part of the rhythm of life. But Lord, let me never get so settled that I close the door to the Spirit's desire to do new things in my life.

THE ASSUMPTION

*I will greatly rejoice in the L*ORD*, my whole being shall exult in my God; for he has clothed me with the garments of salvation, he has covered me with the robe of righteousness. (Isaiah 61:10)*

Lord, when I think of your Mother being taken body and soul into heaven I am reminded of her special place in salvation's plan. I am grateful for such a model of faith and surrender. I rejoice in having such a heavenly mother who loves me, hears me, and wishes always to bring me closer to you, her Son, the answer to all my longings. Mother Mary, watch over me and pray for me now and at the hour of my death.

THE CORONATION

A great portent appeared in heaven: a woman clothed with the sun, with the moon under her feet, and on her head a crown of twelve stars. (Revelation 12:1)

Lord, your Mother's crowning is a reminder to me of your promise of a crown of glory for all who remain faithful to you. This seems too good to be true, yet I believe that you will not forget your word. And so, I turn now to your Mother and pray: Dearest Mary, Heavenly Queen, intercede for me that I may be granted the grace I need daily to remain true to my calling in Jesus. And when I die, lead me to the crown of life that I may share with you the joy and peace of God's reign.

THE LUMINOUS MYSTERIES

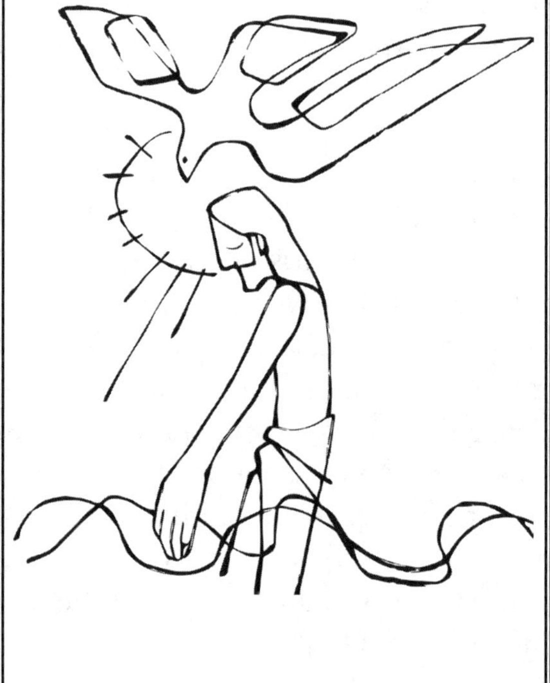

THE BAPTISM OF JESUS

And when Jesus had been baptized,… suddenly the heavens were opened to him and he saw the Spirit of God descending like a dove and alighting on him. And a voice from heaven said, "This is my Son, the Beloved, with whom I am well pleased." (Matthew 3:16–17)

Lord, you are the loving son of a loving father. Love has drawn me to you, Lord, because love is what you are all about. You are, in fact, love. Your Word has said it. I believe it to be true. Teach me to love you and my brothers and sisters without reservation. Teach me to love without fear. Teach me to love as you love me. Teach me to love.

THE WEDDING AT CANA

Jesus said to them, "Fill the jars with water." And they filled them up to the brim. He said to them, "Now draw some out, and take it to the chief steward." So they took it. [Then] the steward tasted the water that had become wine. (John 2:7–9)

Lord, the wine servers did your will without question. And so, today I ask that you grant me the desire to open my heart to the grace of your word—the word you have spoken all along—that it is in doing your will that I receive what I seek; it is in doing your will that life's truth is found.

THE PROCLAMATION OF THE KINGDOM

These twelve Jesus sent out with the following instructions: … "As you go, proclaim the good news, 'The kingdom of heaven has come near.' Cure the sick, raise the dead, cleanse the lepers, cast out demons. You received without payment; give without payment." (Matthew 10:5, 7–8)

Lord, your disciples were called to proclaim the kingdom of God. I need a strong call from you to venture beyond comfortable expectations into the unknown which your resurrection calls me. Let me hear that call as an invitation of love, because it is love alone that has the power to smooth the way for vulnerability and risk-taking.

THE TRANSFIGURATION OF JESUS

And while he was praying, the appearance of his face changed, and his clothes became dazzling white. Then from the cloud came a voice that said, "This is my Son, my Chosen; listen to him!" (Luke 9:29, 35)

Lord, sometimes when I gaze at the sky, time, which in these later years has come to move so quickly, seems, all of a sudden, to stand perfectly still. And for just a moment I rest at the edge of endless possibilities, and I am awed by the wonder of all that has come forth as gifts from your hands. How great are you beyond all I can imagine! How graced are we whom you have made your own!

Then [Jesus] took a loaf of bread, and when he had given thanks, he broke it and gave it to them, saying, "This is my body, which is given for you. Do this in remembrance of me." And he did the same with the cup after supper, saying, "This cup that is poured out for you is the new covenant in my blood."(Luke 22:19–20)

Lord, there is something wonderful about presence. When people share themselves and not just their words, the moment together is charged and blessed with tremendous creative possibilities. Presence is what I do truly desire—the giving of my own presence to you and the experiencing of your presence deep within my heart.